DATE DUE			
OCT 0 4 2012			
DEC 1 1 2012			

DEMCO 38-297

Lemonade

and Other Poems Squeezed from a Single Word

by **Bob Raczka**

illustrated by
Nancy Doniger

Roaring Brook Press

New York

Published by Roaring Brook Press
Roaring Brook Press is a division of Holtzbrinck Publishing Holdings
Limited Partnership
175 Fifth Avenue, New York, New York 10010
mackids.com

"rain" first published in from *i to iran* (IZEN, 1990)
used with the permission of Andrew Russ

Library of Congress Cataloging-in-Publication Data

Raczka, Bob
  Lemonade, and other poems squeezed from a single word / Bob
Raczka; illustrations by Nancy Doniger. —1st ed.
    p. cm.
  ISBN: 978-1-59643-541-4
  1. Children's poetry, American.—I. Doniger, Nancy, ill.—II.
Title.
  PS3618.A346L46 2010
  811'.6—dc22

                                                    2010024807

Roaring Brook Press books are available for
special promotions and premiums.
For details contact: Director of Special Markets,
Holtzbrinck Publishers.

First Edition 2011
Text design by Stephanie Bart-Horvath
Printed in China by South China Printing Company Ltd.,
Dongguan City, Guangdong Province
5 7 9 8 6 4

CONTENTS

I love playing with words. That's why I write
poems.

I also love to see how other people play with
words. That's why I read poems.

One day I was reading about poems on the
Internet, and I came across the poetry of Andrew
Russ. Andrew makes poems out of single words.
Here's my favorite:

                    rain

                     i
                  ra n
                  in

As you can see, Andrew used "rain" as his title,
and then he wrote three more words using only the
letters from the word "rain."

And what a poem! In just three short words, in
just six letters, Andrew has captured how rain
makes us feel.

You probably noticed that the letters in
Andrew's poem are oddly spaced. That's because he
lined up each letter in his poem under the same
letter in his title. This not only makes his poem
more interesting to look at, it proves that he is
sticking to his rule of using only the letters in
his title word.

After I discovered one-word poems, I just had
to try writing some for myself. I hope you enjoy
them and even try to write your own.

                              Bob

lemonade

m   ade
  on   e
    ad

      ad
      de
      d

    on   e
    lemon
    l o ad

        a
      n d

      on   e

      mo
      m

<u>lemonade</u>

made
one
ad

added
one
lemon
load

and
one
mom

```
            bleachers

         b       a
          l
          l


                    r
                   e
            ache  s

                her
                   e

         b   a       s
                 e  s

                  c
            lea    r

                che
                   ers
```

<u>bleachers</u>

ball
reaches
here

bases
clear

cheers

moonlight

                h
    o   t

        n ight

                    t
                    h
                i
        n

            light

        mo   t
                    h
                i
            n

        mo   t
                i
            on

<u>moonlight</u>

hot
night

thin
light

moth
in
motion

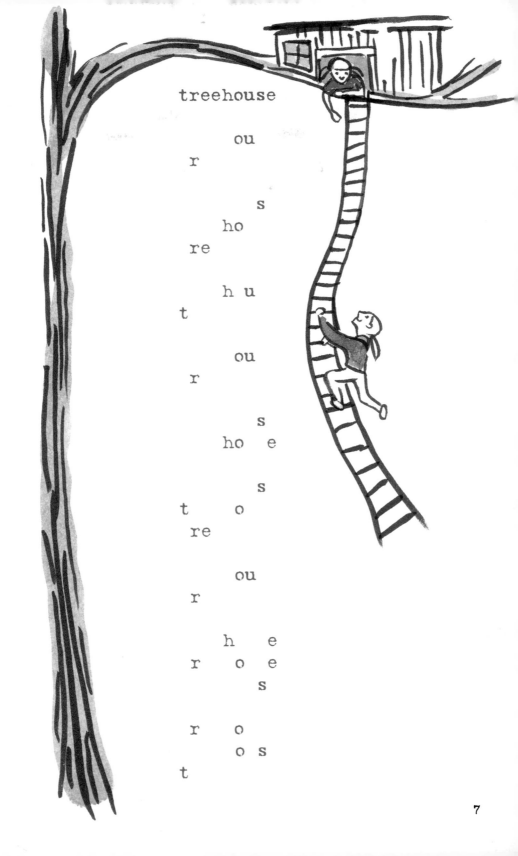

treehouse

       ou
   r
      s
    ho
   re
    h u
 t
     ou
   r
      s
    ho e
      s
 t   o
 re
     ou
   r
     h e
   r o e
      s
   r   o
     o s
 t

treehouse

our
shore
hut

our
shoe
store

our
heroes
roost

```
vacation

  ac tion
       i n
      a
va      n
```

vacation

action
in
a
van

constellation

a

s i

l

e

n t

l ion

tell

s

a n

a

n

c i

e

n t

t

a

l

e

constellation

a
silent
lion
tells
an
ancient
tale

```
        breakfast

        a   f    t
        e
        r

        re       st

        ea       t
        fast
              as
        a
   b   ea    st
```

breakfast

after
rest

eat
fast
as
a
beast

friends

fr e d
f i nds
  e d

<u>friend</u>

fred
finds
ed

playground

```
        r un
    a   round
    a      nd
play
    l      ou d
    la     nd
```

<u>playground</u>

run
around
and
play
loud
land

ladybug

        a

            bug
                g
        y

            bu
    d
    dy

        a

                g
    lad

                g
        a
    l

ladybug

a
buggy
buddy

a
glad
gal

minivan

    ivan

  in

      a
     va

  in

    i an

  in

mi   a

  in

   n an

  in

    an
     n
    a

  in

<u>minivan</u>

ivan
in

ava
in

ian
in

mia
in

nan
in

anna
in

halloween

   all

   al o   n
         e

    a   n

     ow
    l

    a

 h ow
  l
   o

 h

    n

   o

<u>halloween</u>

all
alone

an
owl

a
howl

oh
no

spaghetti

          pa
          pa

               h
            a
       s

            a

          pa
       s   t
            a
              a
          p
          p   et i
                      t
                  e

               he
                      e
            a   t
       s
                  he
            a
          p
       s

spaghetti

papa
has
a
pasta
appetite

he
eats
heaps

creative

        i

cr a   ve

     a

r   t

<u>creative</u>

i
crave
art

snowflakes

a

f　　e
w

flakes

f　a
l
l

a

n　　　e
w

s
e
a
s　o
n

a
w　akes

snowflakes

a
few
flakes
fall

a
new
season
awakes

chocolate

h   at

co at

h o t
c oco a

<u>chocolate</u>

hat

coat

hot
cocoa

television
          s
        e
      t

        is

          on

            i

            s

            i

      t

<u>television</u>

set
is
on

i
sit

```
pepperoni

        on
     e

     p        i
     e

              n
        o

pepper

        n
        o

        oni
        on
```

<u>pepperoni</u>

one
pie

no
pepper

no
onion

```
bicycles

  i
    cycle
b   y
    cy

    cy
    cycles
b   y
  i

bicycle
  cycles
```

bicycles

i
cycle
by
cy

cy
cycles
by
i

bicycle
cycles

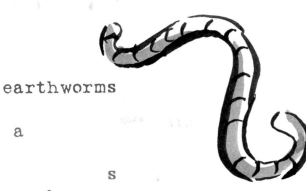

earthworms

     a

         s

      h or

      t

         s

      t orm

       worms

         h

    e r

    e

       worms

      th

    e r

    e

        w

    ear

           s

      h o

    e   s

<u>earthworms</u>

a
short
storm

worms
here

worms
there

wear
shoes

```
            spring

               i
        s    ing

               i
        sp  in

               i
                  g
        rin
```

spring

i
sing

i
spin

i
grin

```
flowers

        we

                s

        low

        f o      r

        f       r
                 e

                 w
        ow    s
```

flowers

we
slow
for
free
wows